MeMe's

FAMILY COOKBOOK

Imperium Publishing
1097 N. 400th Rd
Baldwin City, KS, 66006
www.imperiumpublishing.com

MeMe's

FAMILY COOKBOOK

In 2009, granddaughter Leslie asked me to make a book of my recipes. She was my inspiration and editor. Now, 11 years later, I have tried to get more copies made as our family has seen a lot of changes—marriages, and now 11 great grandchildren. I wanted to add new recipes and correct some old ones, but finding a way to do it seemed impossible until one Sunday afternoon in August 2020 when an old friend and working buddy brought his wife Carol over for a pie-baking school. While talking about my wish to redo my book, Greg Howard told me about a new bookstore in Baldwin Kansas—The Nook and it's owner Niki Manbeck. That Sunday turned out to be a real blessing, and now I'm able to supply my family, including 11 great grandchildren, with a memory book of pictures and recipes. Love all of you so much. Merry Christmas.

Love you all,
MeMe

Main Dishes

Christmas Shrimp

Peel and devein shrimp.
Melt ½ stick of butter in a skillet.
Add ¼ tsp garlic salt or powder.
Add shrimp and simmer 5 to 10 minutes while turning shrimp.

Optional:
Wrap large shrimp with ¼ slice of bacon.
Place on a baking sheet.

Bake at 350° for 30 minutes or until bacon is done.

Hamburger Corn Muffin Casserole

Mix as directed:
2 Jiffy corn muffin mixes

Add: 1 can cream corn.

Brown:
1 lb hamburger
1 clove garlic
½ cup chopped onions

Add: 1 can Ro-Tel tomatoes.

Spray 9x12 pan. Spread half of the cornbread mix. Layer hamburger mix. Cover with remaining half of the cornbread mix. Cover with shredded cheese.

Bake 350° for 40 minutes.

Meat Loaf

2 lbs hamburger (or 1 lb ground pork or deer burger)
2 eggs
1 cup evaporated milk
1 small onion chopped
2 cups quick-cook oatmeal
1 Tbsp chili powder
1 Tbsp garlic powder
2 tsp salt
½ tsp pepper

Mix well and shape into a 9x13 pan.

Top with a mixture of:
½ cup ketchup
¼ cup brown sugar

Bake at 350° for 1 hour.

Chicken Pot Pie Bubble

Mix together:
2 cups chicken shredded
1 cup sour cream
1 cup canned chicken soup
1 cup cheddar cheese
1 bag frozen veggies
1 tsp garlic powder
½ tsp salt
2 6-oz cans biscuits cut in ¼ pieces

Place in 9x13 dish.
Bake at 375° for 35 to 45 minutes.

How to Bake a Ham

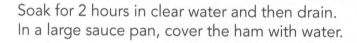 (I use Cook's bone-in hams.)

Soak for 2 hours in clear water and then drain. In a large sauce pan, cover the ham with water.

Add:
1 cup vinegar
¾ cup brown sugar.

Parboil until tender 1½ to 2 hours depending on the size of the ham. Drain and cut off rind.

Make a "paste" of:
1 tsp ground cloves
¾ cups brown sugar
1 Tbsp flour
¼ cup water

Spread paste on the ham and place in a backing pan.

Add: 2 cups of ginger ale or 7up.

Bake at 325° for 1 hour.

Meat, Potatoes and Gravy

Use round steak, pork steak or pork chops (whatever quantity necessary)
2 Tbsp oil
½ cup flour
1 can cream of mushroom soup
1½ cups milk
Potatoes peeled and quartered (whatever quantity necessary)

Heat oil in skillet. Cover meat with flour and brown. Place potatoes on top of meat. Mix soup and milk and pour over the top. Salt and pepper to taste.

This can all be done in an electric skillet or put in a 9x13 pan or roaster.

Cover and simmer 1 hour in electric skillet or bake at 350° for 1 hour.

Chicken on Sunday

1⅓ cups minute rice
1 can cream of celery soup
1 can cream of mushroom soup
½ cup milk
1 envelope dry onion soup mix
1 frying chicken cut up or 4 chicken breasts

Grease a 9x13 baking dish and sprinkle rice evenly over the bottom. Heat cream of celery and mushroom with milk until blended. Pour over rice. Top with chicken. Sprinkle onion soup mix over chicken. Cover with foil.

Bake at 325° for 2 hours.

Brisket ← (6 to 8 pounds)

Marinate brisket overnight with a bottle of Italian dressing. Place brisket in foil or covered baking dish. Pour marinade over the brisket.

Bake at 300° for 4 hours or until done.

Cool. Trim off fat and slice meat against the grain.

Mix together and heat:
1 pint of Meme's homemade chili sauce
1 cup of KC Masterpiece BBQ sauce

Pour over brisket and bake at 350° for 30 minutes.

Pork Roast

(3 to 4 pounds)

Marinade:
½ cup chopped onions
¼ cup chicken both
¼ cup vinegar
2 Tbsp olive oil
4 garlic cloves or 1 tsp garlic powder
¼ tsp black pepper
⅓ cup soy sauce
2 Tbsp Worcestershire sauce

Mix all ingredients together and put in plastic bag with roast. Marinate 4 to 8 hours.

Add: 2 cups chicken broth to marinade sauce.

Place in roaster and bake uncovered at 350° for 2½ hours.

Oven Fried Chicken

1 whole chicken cut up or a number of breasts
2 cups flour
1 tsp season salt
¼ tsp black pepper
2 cups buttermilk
olive oil or peanut oil

In a plastic bag, soak chicken 30 minutes in buttermilk. In separate bowl, mix flour, season salt, and pepper. Coat chicken in flour mixture. Brown chicken in skillet with olive oil or peanut oil. Place chicken in 9x13 pan.

Bake at 350° for 45 minutes.

Indian Tacos

(Makes 4 tacos)

Fried bread:
2 cups self-rising flour
1 to 1½ cups buttermilk to make a soft dough
2 Tbsp honey
Peanut oil

Mix together to form dough. Divide in 4 equal parts. Working on floured board, flatten to ¼ inch thick and 6 to 8 inch circles. Heat 1 to 2 inches of peanut oil to 300° in an electric skillet. Using a spatula, lift bread into hot oil. Cook 1 to 2 minutes or until light brown on both sides. Remove and pat with paper towel.

Top with refried

Mexican Casserole

2 lbs hamburger
1 onion chopped
1 can cream of mushroom soup
1 can chili beans
½ lb Velveeta cheese
1 bell pepper chopped
1 can green chilies
2 jalapenos chopped
1 can tomato sauce
Corn tortillas

Brown hamburger, onion and peppers. Drain. Add soup, tomato sauce and beans. Place layers of tortillas in 9x13 baking dish. Cover with ½ the meat mixture and ½ the cheese. Repeat layers.

Bake at 350° for 30 minutes.

Taco Salad

Brown:
1½ lbs ground beef
½ cup shopped onion
1 Tbsp chili powder

Melt:
1 lb Velveeta cheese
combined with Ro-Tel
tomatoes

Mix:
Shredded lettuce
Chopped tomatoes
Frito corn chips

Top with meat mixture
and cheese, then toss.

Cream Can Dinner

Layer into can:
1 clean 10-gallon milk can
36 ears of sweet corn, shucks on, ends cut off
6 pounds new red potatoes
4 pounds carrots scraped and cut in large hunks
1 large head of cabbage cut into chunks
3 pounds whole onions cleaned
5 pounds polish sausage

Pour 6 cans of beer over ingredients. Tie down lid with wire.
Cook on outdoor cooker for 30 minutes after steam begins.
Empty into large container and serve.

Hamburger Soup

1 lb hamburger browned and drained
1 8-oz can tomato sauce
1 tsp sugar
3 large carrots peeled and sliced
1 large potato peeled and cubed
1 envelope Lipton onion soup mix
1 14-oz can tomatoes
2 cups water
½ tsp pepper
1 14-oz can green beans not drained

Mix all ingredients and simmer 1 hour.

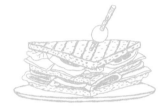

Reuben Sandwich

1 lb sliced corned beef
4 large slices of Swiss
    cheese or 8 regular slices
1 14-oz can drained sauerkraut (I use Frank's Sweet Kraut with
    caraway seeds)
8 slices pumpernickel or any dark bread

Spread 4 slices of bread with butter. Place on 300° grill or in
skillet. Top with ¼ of corned beef, 1 slice of Swiss cheese, ¼
of the sauerkraut, and second slice of buttered bread. Turn
sandwich over when browned and cook until cheese melts.

BBQ Meat Balls

1 13-oz can evaporated milk
3 lbs ground beef
2 cups oatmeal
2 eggs
1 cup onions
½ tsp pepper
2 tsp salt
2 tsp chili powder
½ tsp garlic powder

Mix together and make 24 meat balls. Cover with sauce.

Bake at 350° for 1½ hours.

Sauce:
2 cups catsup
1½ cup brown sugar
2 tsp liquid smoke
½ tsp garlic powder
½ cup onion

Beef Porcupines

1 lb ground beef
½ cup long grain rice
2 tsp salt
¼ tsp celery salt
1 Tbsp onion
2 Tbsp chopped green pepper
1 small clove garlic chopped
1 Tbsp Worcestershire sauce

Mix and form into balls.

Bring to boil:
4 cups of tomato juice
½ tsp Tabasco sauce
1 Tbsp sugar

Place meat balls in juice and simmer 1 hour.

Breakfast Casserole

2 cups soft bread cut into 1 inch squares
1¾ cup milk to soak bread
8 slightly beaten eggs
¾ tsp salt
½ lb Swiss cheese shredded
½ cup dry bread crumbs
4 Tbsp butter or margarine
⅛ tsp pepper
8 slices bacon fried and crumbled

Soak bread crumbs in milk, drain ,and add milk to the beaten eggs. Melt 2 Tbsp butter in skillet and scramble eggs over low heat until soft. Add salt, pepper and bread. Put eggs in 9-inch square dish. Top with shredded cheese. Melt last 2 Tbsp butter, mix with bread crumbs. Put on top of cheese. Sprinkle bacon on top.

Bake at 400° for 10 minutes.

Sides and Salads

Baked Macaroni and Cheese

½ stick of margarine or butter
1 tsp salt
2½ cups uncooked macaroni
4 cups milk
1½ cups cubed Velveeta or grated cheese

In a sauce pan, melt butter, then stir in salt and macaroni. Add milk and cheese. Heat until cheese melts. Put in lightly-greased 2-qt casserole dish.

Bake at 325° for at least 1 hour.

Zucchini Casserole

4 cups zucchini sliced thin
1 medium onion chopped

Stir-fry in 2 Tbsp olive oil until crisp and tender.

Add:
1 14 oz can tomatoes
    drained
½ tsp salt
¼ tsp pepper
¼ tsp garlic powder
½ tsp oregano

Simmer 10 minutes. Top with 1 to 2 cups shredded cheese and heat until melted.

I use an electric skillet for this, but you can fix in a skillet on the stove and put in a baking dish.

Bake at 350° for 30 minutes.

Creamed Asparagus

4 cups cut asparagus
1 tsp salt
1 cup water

Cook until tender, then drain.

Add:
1 cup milk
½ cup non-dairy creamer or half and half
2 Tbsp cornstarch dissolved in ¼ cup milk
1 Tbsp butter

Cook over low hear until thick.

Deviled Eggs

Put 6 eggs in saucepan and cover with cold water. Add 1 tsp salt to water and bring to a full boil. Turn off heat, cover pan, and let set for 15 minutes. Cool eggs with cold water. Peel and cut lengthwise.

Put yolks in bowl and smash with a fork.
Add:
3 Tbsp mayo
¼ tsp salt
1 tsp mustard
2 tsp sugar

Mix until fluffy. Fill egg white halves with yolk mixture. Sprinkle with paprika.

Jalapeno Poppers

2 lbs jalapeno peppers
½ lb bacon

Mix:
8 oz cream cheese
6 oz Parmesan cheese grated
¼ tsp garlic salt
¼ tsp chili pepper

Slice peppers in half lengthwise and take out seeds. Fill with cream cheese mixture. Put on baking sheet and lay 3 inch piece of bacon over each filled pepper.

Bake at 375° for 30 minutes or until bacon is cooked.

Fresh Spinach Salad

Mix:
1 lb fresh spinach
1 can or 2 cups bean sprouts rinsed
 and drained
1 can sliced water chestnuts
 drained
4 hard-boiled eggs sliced
1 cup fresh mushrooms sliced
3 chopped green onions
½ lb bacon fried and crumbled

Dressing:
¾ cup sugar
¼ cup oil
¼ cup vinegar
⅓ cup catsup
2 tsp salt
1 tsp Worcestershire sauce

Seven Layer Salad

(Serves 8 to 10)

small head of lettuce shredded
½ cup chopped green pepper
1 10-oz pkg frozen peas thawed
½ cup chopped celery
½ cup chopped onion
2 Tbsp sugar
6 oz grated cheese
8 slices bacon crumbled

Mix:
½ cup mayo
1½ cup sour cream

Layer lettuce, pepper, celery, peas and onions. Spoon mayo
mixture over salad like frosting. Sprinkle with sugar. Top with
cheese and bacon. Cover and chill overnight. Do not stir.

Japanese Salad

4 cups chopped cabbage or 1 pkg slaw
3 green onions chopped
1 pkg ramen noodles—chicken flavored (save flavor packet
    for dressing)
⅔ cup roasted sunflower seeds
½ cup toasted slivered almonds

Dressing:
⅓ cup vegetable oil
⅓ cup brown sugar
3 tsp vinegar dash of garlic salt
Flavor packet from ramen noodles

In a large bowl mix slaw, green onion, sunflower seeds and almonds. In a small bowl, mix brown sugar, oil, vinegar garlic salt and seasoning packet from noodles. Pour sauce over salad mix. Just before serving break ramen noodles into small pieces and mix into salad.

Fruit Salad

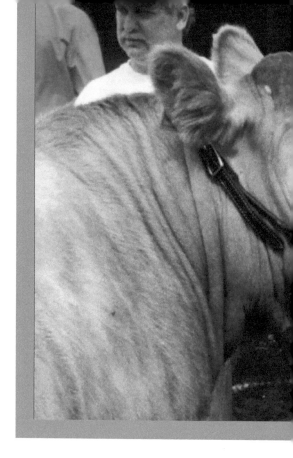

1 20-oz can pineapple chunks
½ cup sugar
2 Tbsp cornstarch
⅓ cup orange juice
1 Tbsp lemon juice
1 11 oz can mandarin oranges drained
2 or 3 bananas
3 or 4 unpeeled apples chopped

Drain pineapple saving ¾ cup of juice. In sauce pan, combine sugar and cornstarch. Add juice and heat over medium heat stirring often until thick and bubbly. Once bubbling, cook 1 minute longer. Set aside. In a bowl, combine all the fruit and pour warm sauce over, stirring gently to coat. Cover and refrigerate.

Coleslaw Apple Salad ← (Makes enough to feed 20 people)

1 medium head cabbage shredded or thinly sliced
3 red delicious apples chopped but not peeled
⅓ cup sugar
½ cup mayo
½ cup sour cream
½ tsp salt
2 Tbsp white vinegar

Mix sugar, mayo, sour cream, salt and vinegar. Pour over cabbage and apples. Toss lightly. Will keep for several days in the refrigerator or you can make the dressing alone and keep in refrigerator for up to two weeks.

Breads

Banana Bread

1 cup ripe banana mashed
⅓ cup shortening
⅔ cup sugar
2 eggs
1¾ cup flour
2 tsp baking powder
¼ tsp baking soda
nuts optional

Mix all together. Pour into loaf pan.

Bake at 350° for 45 minutes to 1 hour.

Pumpkin Bread (Two loaves)

1 tsp baking soda
1 tsp salt
1 tsp cinnamon
2 cups sugar
4 beaten eggs
2 cups pumpkin (1 can)
1½ cups salad oil

Put all dry ingredients in a bowl. Add wet ingredients, stir carefully just enough to dampen. Pour in greased loaf pan.

Bake at 350° for 1 hour.

Corn Bread ⤆ (Good and Easy)

2 boxes Jiffy cornbread mixed
    according to directions
1 box Jiffy yellow cake mixed
    according to directions

Mix the two together. Pour into a
9x13 pan.

Bake at 400° for 20 minutes or
until light brown and toothpick
comes out clean.

(Makes 2 loaves or 4 small pans)

Zucchini Bread

¾ cup vegetable oil
1¼ cup sugar
1¾ cup shredded zucchini
3 eggs
2 cups all purpose flour
1¼ tsp baking soda
2½ tsp baking powder
1 tsp salt
1 tsp cinnamon
nuts/raisins optional

Combine oil, sugar, eggs and zucchini in a large bowl. Mix remaining ingredients together. Gradually add to zucchini mixture. Beat 3 minutes with mixer. Pour in greased and flour-coated pans.

Bake at 325° for 1 hour.

Best Ever Biscuits

2 cups flour
4 tsp baking powder
½ tsp cream of tartar
½ tsp salt
2 Tbsp sugar
½ cup shortening (butter-flavored Crisco is great for this)
1 egg slightly beaten
⅔ cups milk

Stir all dry ingredients together. Cut in shortening. Add milk and then egg last. Stir well. Dough will be sticky. Turn out dough onto floured board and knead about 5 times gently. Roll out ½ inch thick and cut.

Bake at 450° for 10 to 15 minutes.

Hot Rolls

(Makes 2 dozen)

2 pkg dry yeast
¼ cup sugar
1 tsp salt
5¼ cups flour
½ cup warm water
1 cup milk
¼ cup margarine (½ stick)
2 eggs beaten

Sprinkle yeast in warm water in mixing bowl. Combine milk, sugar, salt and margarine. Mix well. Add yeast and the beaten egg. Stir in 2 cups flour. Mix well. Add remaining flour to make stiff dough. Knead dough 5 minutes. Place in greased bowl and let rest 1½ hours. Let rise until doubled. Turn dough out onto a floured board. Kneed 15 to 20 times. Make into individual rolls and place on greased cookie sheet or into muffin pans. Let rise again until doubled.

Bake at 400° for 15 to 20 minutes.

Cakes, Cookies, Desserts & Pies

Angel Food Cake

1 cup cake flour
1½ cup powdered sugar
1½ cup egg whites
½ tsp salt
1 cup sugar
1½ tsp cream of tartar
1 tsp almond extract
½ tsp vanilla

Sift cake flour and powdered sugar together 3 times and set aside. Beat egg whites, salt and cream of tartar until foamy. Add sugar very slowly while beating. Beat until very stiff peaks form. Add almond extract and vanilla. Fold in flour, powdered sugar mixture slowly with a large wooden spoon. Put dough in tube pan and drop on counter 3 times, and run a long knife around and through dough to remove all air holes.

Bake on bottom rack of oven at 350° for 45 minutes. Invert pan and cool before removing the cake.

Texas Sheet Cake

2 cups sugar
2 cups flour
1 tsp baking soda
1 cup hot water
2 sticks margarine (1 cup)
4 Tbsp unsweetened cocoa
2 eggs
½ cup buttermilk or sour cream
1 tsp vanilla

Mix sugar, flour and baking soda. In a sauce pan, bring water, margarine and cocoa to a boil. Pour over flour mixture and mix well. Add eggs, buttermilk and vanilla. Pour batter into a 13x9x2 inch jelly roll pan greased and floured.

Bake at 350° for 25 minutes or until toothpick comes out clean.

Frosting:
1 stick margarine
4 Tbsp cocoa
1 lb powdered sugar
6 Tbsp milk
1 tsp vanilla
½ cup chopped nuts (optional)

In a sauce pan, melt margarine. Add cocoa and milk. Bring to a boil. Stir in powdered sugar, vanilla and nuts. Spread on cake while it is still warm.

Coffee Cake

1 small potato cooked and mashed
2 cups milk
1 cup potato water
1 cup sugar
1 tsp lemon extract
1 tsp vanilla
1 egg
2 pkgs yeast
1 cup raisins
1 Tbsp salt
8 cups flour

Mix all ingredients. Let rise until doubled, work down, let rise again. Divide dough into 4 equal parts. Shape into loaves. Place on 2 greased cookie sheets. Brush tops with melted butter and sprinkle with cinnamon and sugar. Let rise until doubled.

Bake at 325° for 30 minutes.

These are delicious and pretty. They make nice Christmas gifts for neighbors and friends.

German Sweet Chocolate Cake

1 pkg (4 oz) Bakers German sweet chocolate
½ cup water
2 cups flour
1 tsp baking soda
¼ tsp salt
4 egg whites
1 cup (2 sticks) butter or margarine softened
2 cups sugar
1 tsp vanilla
1 cup buttermilk
4 egg yolks

Line bottoms of three 9 inch round cake pans with wax paper. Microwave chocolate and water in bowl. Stir until melted. Sift together flour, baking soda and salt. Beat butter and sugar in large bowl with mixer on medium until light and fluffy. Add yolks 1 at a time, beating in each addition. Stir in chocolate mixture and vanilla. Add flour mixture alternately with buttermilk, beating again after each addition until smooth. Beat egg whites in another bowl with mixer on high until stiff peaks form. Gently stir into batter. Pour into prepared pan.

Bake at 350° for 30 minutes or until toothpick comes out clean.

Cool 15 minutes before removing from pans. Spread frosting between layers and over the top of cake.

Frosting:
1 can evaporated milk
1½ cups sugar
4 egg yolks
1½ tsp vanilla
¾ cup butter
2⅔ cups coconut
1½ cups chopped pecans

Mix milk, sugar, egg yolks and vanilla
in large sauce pan. Cook and stir on
medium heat about 12 minutes or until
thickened and golden brown. Remove
from heat. Stir in coconut and pecans.
Cool to room temperature.

Cake Mixes Made Better

To any cake mix add:
3 eggs (whites only for white cake mixes)
½ cup oil
buttermilk instead of water

Bake as directed on box.

Blueberry Dessert

3 cups graham cracker crumbs
½ cup margarine melted
3 Tbsp granulated sugar
1 pint blueberries
⅔ cup granulated sugar
2 Tbsp corn starch
⅓ cup water
1 pkg of Dream Whip
8 oz cream cheese
3 Tbsp powdered sugar

Cook blueberries, ⅔ cup sugar, water and corn starch in a small pan until thick. Cool completely. Mix cracker crumbs and 3 Tbsp granulated sugar with melted margarine. Press crust into an 8x11 pan. Mix Dream Whip according to directions, then add cream cheese and powdered sugar. Mix well. Spread Dream Whip mixture over crust, then top with cooled blueberry mixture. Cover and put in refrigerator for 3 to 4 hours. Cut in squares and serve.

Red, White and Blue Dessert

1 angel food cake
2 pkg instant vanilla pudding
3 cups milk
8-oz container of Cool Whip
1 quart fresh strawberries cut in half
1 pint fresh blueberries

Mix instant pudding and milk. Fold in Cool Whip. Cut angel food into small pieces. In a 9x13 pan, layer ½ of the cake pudding, strawberries and blueberries, then repeat layers. Refrigerate. Can be made the day before or several hours before serving.

No Bake Cookies

2 cups sugar
½ cup milk
1 stick of margarine
⅓ cup cocoa

Bring these ingredients to a rolling boil. Boil 1 minute.
Do not overcook.

Immediately add:
½ cup peanut butter
3 cups quick oatmeal

Spoon onto wax paper and let cool.

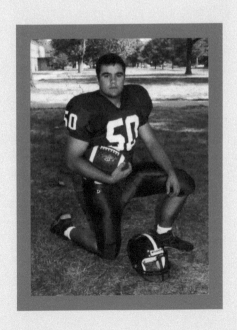

Easy Cookies

1 box cake mix (any kind)
2 eggs
½ cup oil

Mix until smooth. Add your choice of raisins, nuts, coconut, chocolate chips or anything you think would be good with the cake mix. Spoon onto cookie sheet.

Bake at 350° for 8 to 10 minutes.

Sugar Cookies (Yields 4 to 5 dozen)

1½ cups powdered sugar
1 cup butter
1 egg
2½ cups sifted flour
1 tsp cream of tartar
1 tsp vanilla
½ tsp almond flavoring

Cream sugar, butter, egg and flavoring. Sift dry ingredients and stir into wet. Refrigerate 3 hours. Once chilled, divide dough in half and roll out on floured surface. Cut and place on cookie sheet

Bake at 370° for 7 to 8 minutes.

Russian Tea Cakes

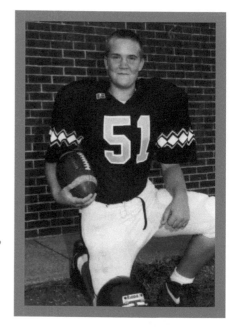

Mix together:
1 cup soft butter
½ cup sifted powdered sugar
1 tsp vanilla

Sift together and stir into butter mixture:
2¼ cups sifted flour
¼ tsp salt
Stir in ¾ cup finely chopped pecans

Chill dough. Roll into 1 inch balls. Place onto ungreased cookie sheet.

Bake at 400° for 10 to 12 minutes.

Coat with powdered sugar, cool and repeat.
Note: Cookies do not spread

Gingerbread Cookies *(Makes 2 dozen)*

3 cups flour
2 tsp ground ginger
1 tsp cinnamon
1 tsp baking soda
¼ tsp nutmeg
¼ tsp salt
¾ cup butter (1½ sticks)
¾ cup brown sugar
½ cup molasses
1 egg
1 tsp vanilla

Sift together dry ingredients except for the brown sugar. Beat butter and sugar together. Add molasses, egg and vanilla. Beat in dry ingredients. Refrigerate 4 hours or overnight. Roll out to ¼ inch thickness.

Bake at 350° for 8 to 10 minutes.

Peanut Butter Fudge

4 cups sugar
1 12-oz can evaporated milk
1 stick margarine or butter
1 7-oz jar of marshmallow fluff
1½ cups peanut butter

Mix sugar, milk and butter. Cook until it forms a soft ball in cold water. Remove from heat. Add peanut butter and fluff. Pour into greased 9x13 pan. Set in refrigerator. When cool, cut into squares.

Peanut Clusters

Place in Crock-Pot and melt:
2 lbs chocolate almond bark
1 lb white almond bark
1 12-oz bag chocolate chips

Add:
2 to 3 cups of salted peanuts (more if desired)

Spoon onto wax paper and allow to cool until set up.

Peanut Butter Blossom Cookies

⅓ cup peanut butter
½ cup sugar
½ cup brown sugar
½ cup butter
1 egg
1 tsp vanilla
1¾ cups flour
½ tsp salt
1 tsp baking soda
Chocolate Kisses

Combine all ingredients except chocolate Kisses. Form dough into balls and roll in sugar.

Bake 350° for 10 minutes.

Remove from oven and push a Kiss into the center of each cookie.

Fool-Proof Pie Crust

(Will make 2 two-crust pies or 4 to 5 pie shells)

4 cups flour
1¾ cup Crisco shortening
1 Tbsp sugar
2 tsp salt
1 Tbsp vinegar
1 egg beaten
½ cup cold water

With fork, mix together flour, sugar, salt and shortening to the size of peas. Combine water, beaten egg, and vinegar. Pour into flour mixture. With your hands, work into a ball. Place into a covered bowl and refrigerate for at least 15 minutes or up to 3 days, or place in freezer. Roll out between wax paper.

"Not everyone wants to make a pie crust, but everyone can make a pie. Buy a frozen or refrigerated crust at the grocery store. Fill it with pumpkin, pecan, or the dutch apple recipe, and bake as directed. Or bake the crust as directed, cool, and fill with your favorite 3 cups of instant pudding and top with Cool Whip." – Grandma

Fresh Strawberry Pie

5 cups fresh strawberries
½ cup water
1 cup sugar
3 Tbsp cornstarch
1 tsp lemon juice
1 Tbsp butter
Drop of red food coloring
1 baked 9-inch pie crust

Crush 2 cups of strawberries. Add water and boil 2 minutes. Strain juice through a tea strainer. To juice, add sugar, cornstarch, lemon juice, butter and coloring. Cook until thick. Cool. Wash and stem 3 cups of fresh berries. Place half in baked pie shell. Pour half of syrup over berries. Then repeat layers with second half of berries and syrup. Cool. Top with whipped cream and garnish with whole berries. Keep refrigerated for at least 3 hours before cutting.

Strawberry Rhubarb Pie

1¼ cup sugar
⅓ cup flour
2 cup fresh strawberries
2 cups chopped rhubarb
2 Tbsp butter
2 Tbsp cornstarch
1½ tsp vanilla
¼ tsp salt
2 unbaked 9-inch pie crusts

Place one pie crust in bottom of pie plate. Mix fruit together in a bowl. Sift sugar and flour together. Mix ¾ of dry mixture with fruit and spread the remaining dry mixture over bottom crust. Add fruit mixture to bottom crust. Dot with butter. Top with second crust.

Bake at 350° for 55 minutes.

Strawberry Crumb Pie

Stir together:
6 cups sliced strawberries
½ cup tapioca
1 cup sugar

Mix together:
1 cup flour
½ cup brown sugar
½ cup butter

Put strawberry mixture in unbaked pie shell.
Top with crumbs (flour mixture).

Bake at 350° for 55 minutes.

Pecan Pie

3 eggs
1 cup Karo light or dark syrup
1 cup sugar
3 Tbsp melted butter or margarine
1 tsp vanilla
1 tsp salt
1½ cups pecans
1 unbaked 9-inch pie shell

Beat eggs slightly in a small bowl with mixer at medium speed. Beat in syrup, sugar, butter, vanilla and salt. Stir in pecans. Pour into pie shell. Cover edges with foil.

Bake at 350° for 60 minutes.

Pumpkin Pie

¾ cup sugar
½ tsp salt
1 tsp cinnamon
1 tsp pumpkin pie spice
2 eggs
1 15-oz can pumpkin
1 12-oz can evaporated milk
1 unbaked 9-inch pie shell

Beat eggs in a large bowl. Add sugar, salt, cinnamon, pumpkin spice and pumpkin. Mix and slowly stir in can of milk. Pour into pie shell. Cover edges with foil .

Bake at 425° for 15 minutes.
Reduce heat to 350° and bake an additional 45 minutes.

Peanut Butter Pie

In a saucepan, combine:
3 Tbsp cornstarch
3 Tbsp flour
1 cup sugar
¼ tsp salt

Beat and add:
3 cups milk
3 egg yolks

Cook over medium heat until thick, stirring often. Remove from heat.

Add:
2 Tbsp butter
½ cup peanut butter (more if desired)
1 tsp vanilla

Pour in baked 9-inch pie shell. Top with meringue and sprinkle with chopped peanuts.

Bake at 350° for 22 minutes.

Apple Pie

6 cups peeled, cored and sliced apples (I use Red Delicious,
    yellow or Jonathan)
½ cup coffee creamer
1 cup sugar
2 Tbsp flour
2 Tbsp cornstarch
2 unbaked 9-inch pie crusts

Mix ingredients together. Place in unbaked pie shell and top
with second crust. Cut a slit or design on top to vent. Cover
edges with foil.

Bake at 350° for 1 hour.

Dutch Apple Pie

5 cups peeled, cored and sliced apples
3 Tbsp cornstarch
¼ tsp cinnamon
½ cup half and half or non dairy creamer
½ cup sugar
1 9-inch unbaked pie shell

Mix ingredients and place in 9-inch unbaked pie shell.

Topping:
½ stick butter softened
1 cup flour
½ cup brown sugar

Mix flour and brown sugar. Cut in butter until crumbly.
Sprinkle over apples. Cover with foil.

Bake at 350° for 55 minutes.

Blackberry- Apple Pie

1 cup blackberries
4 cups peeled and sliced apples
2 Tbsp cornstarch
2 Tbsp flour
½ tsp cinnamon
1 cup sugar
½ cup coffee creamer
2 unbaked 9-inch pie crusts

Mix ingredients and place in an unbaked
9-inch pie shell. Top with second crust. Cover
edges with foil.

Bake at 350° for 1 hour.

Blackberry Pie

4 cups blackberries
1¼ cup sugar
½ cup flour
1 tsp cinnamon
2 Tbsp butter
2 unbaked 9-inch pie crusts

Mix ingredients together. Pour into unbaked pie shell.
Top with second crust. Cover edges with foil.

Bake at 350° for 1 hour.

Peach-Blackberry Pie

3 cups sliced peaches
1 cup blackberries
1 cup sugar
½ tsp cinnamon
2 Tbsp cornstarch
1 Tbsp flour
2 Tbsp butter

Mix ingredients and pour into unbaked 9-inch pie shell. Top with second crust. Cover edges with foil.

Bake at 350° for 1 hour.

Peach Pie

4 cups peeled peaches (5 or 6 large peaches)
1 cup sugar
3 Tbsp cornstarch
⅛ tsp cinnamon
½ cup water
½ tsp almond extract
1 Tbsp butter
2 9-inch unbaked pie crusts

Slice 2 cups of peaches and place in unbaked pie shell. In a saucepan, crush 2 cups of peaches and add sugar, cornstarch, cinnamon and water. Stir in almond extract and butter. Cook until thick and clear. Pour over sliced peaches. Top with second crust.

Bake at 350° for 55 minutes.

Cherry Pie

4 cups sour cherries
¾ cup cherry juice
¼ cup cornstarch
1 Tbsp butter
¾ tsp almond extract
1½ cups sugar
2 unbaked 9-inch pie crusts

Drain cherries. In saucepan, put cherry juice, ¾ cup sugar and cornstarch. Bring to a boil and cook until thick. Add ½ cup of sugar, almond and butter. Fold in cherries. Put in unbaked pie shell and top with second crust.

Bake at 350° for 45 minutes.

Pie Meringue (Use on cream pies)

5 egg whites
¼ tsp salt
1 tsp cream of tartar

Beat until foamy.

Slowly add: ½ cup sugar.

Continue beating until very stiff peaks form, at least 3 minutes after the last of the sugar is added. Seal edges of the pie with the meringue.

Bake at 350° for 20 to 22 minutes.

Coconut Cream Pie

In a heavy sauce pan, combine:
¾ cup sugar
¼ tsp salt
3 Tbsp flour
3 Tbsp cornstarch

Beat together and gradually add:
3 cups milk
3 egg yolks

Cook over medium heat, stirring constantly, until mixture boils and thickens. Remove from heat.

Add:
2 Tbsp butter
½ cup coconut
½ tsp coconut extract
1 tsp vanilla

Pour in baked 9-inch pie shell. Top with meringue. Sprinkle with coconut.

Bake at 350° for 20 minutes.

Best-Ever Lemon Pie

1¼ cups sugar
6 Tbsp cornstarch
2 cups water
⅓ cup lemon juice
3 egg yolks
1½ tsp lemon extract
1 tsp vinegar
3 Tbsp butter
1 baked 9-inch pie shell

Mix sugar and cornstarch together in the top of a double boiler. Add 2 cups water. Combine egg yolks and lemon juice and beat well. Add to the sugar mixture. Cook over boiling water until thick (about 20 minutes). Add extract, vinegar and butter. Stir thoroughly. Pour into baked pie crust. Cover with meringue.

Bake at 350° for 20 minutes.

Chocolate Pie

In a saucepan, combine:
3 Tbsp cornstarch
3 Tbsp flour
1 cup sugar
3 Tbsp unsweetened cocoa
¼ tsp salt

Beat and add:
3 cups milk
3 egg yolks

Cook over medium heat until thick, stirring often. Remove from heat.

Add:
2 Tbsp butter
1 tsp vanilla
½ tsp almond extract

Pour in baked 9-inch pie shell. Top with meringue and sprinkle with mini chocolate bits.

Bake at 350° for 22 minutes.

Butterscotch Pie

In a saucepan, combine:
3 Tbsp cornstarch
3 Tbsp flour
1 cup brown sugar
¼ tsp salt

Beat and add:
3 cups milk
3 egg yolks

Cook over medium heat until thick, stirring often. Remove from heat.

Add:
2 Tbsp butter
1 tsp vanilla
¼ tsp maple extract

Pour in baked 9-inch pie shell. Top with meringue and sprinkle with butterscotch morsels.

Bake at 350° for 22 minutes.

Miscellaneous

Homemade Vanilla Ice Cream

(Yields 1 gallon)

2 cups sugar
4 beaten eggs
1 Tbsp vanilla
¼ tsp salt
1 qt heavy whipping cream
2½ qts milk

Mix together. Freeze in ice.

Salsa 🍅

22 medium tomatoes
5-20 jalapeno peppers (to desired taste)
5 medium onions
1 6-oz can of tomato paste
¾ cup sugar
2 green peppers
¼ cup salt
1 cup vinegar

Peel and chop tomatoes, jalapenos (remove seeds), green peppers and onions. Add other ingredients. Bring to a boil. Simmer 1½ hours. Fill pint jars. Process 10 minutes at 5 lbs pressure or hot water bath for 20 minutes.

Chili Sauce

Mix together:
3 qts tomatoes peeled and chopped
1 cup chopped green peppers
¼ cup salt
2 cups chopped onions
3 cups chopped celery

Let stand 6 to 8 hours. Drain (freeze or can juice to use in chili and vegetable stews).

Add:
1 cup white vinegar
1½ tsp mixed pickling spices
2 cups sugar
1½ tsp black pepper
¼ cup brown sugar

Bring all to a boil and let simmer for 15 minutes. Put in jars, seal and process 10 minutes at 5 lbs pressure or hot water bath for 20 minutes.

Thad Allender/Journal-World Photo

LAWRENCE'S BRAD HARRELL, LEFT, and Topeka's Russell Washington wrestle for position.

Horseradish Pickles

1 qt jar kosher whole dill pickles
⅔ cup vinegar
⅓ cup water
2 cups sugar
2½ oz prepared horseradish

Drain off juice from pickles and rinse with water. Cut into chunks and put back into empty jar. In a sauce pan, add vinegar and water, heat until boiling. Slowly stir in sugar and bring to a boil. Put horseradish over pickles in the jar. Pour hot, clear liquid over horseradish and pickles. Refrigerate for at least 1 week. Stir or flip jar to mix juices during the week.

Freezer Corn

6 cups of sweet corn kernels (Clean ears of corn and cut
 kernels off cob).
2 tsp salt
3 tsp sugar
1 cup hot water

Bring to a boil and cook 2 minutes. Cool corn by putting pan
in sink of cold water. When cool, bag corn and freeze. To use,
heat and add butter.

Sweet Lime Pickles (Crisp and good)

7 lbs cucumbers cut in chunks
2 gallons water
2 cups lime

Soak 24 hours, then wash in 2 separate clear waters.

Heat:
4½ lbs (10½ cups) sugar
1 Tbsp whole cloves
1 Tbsp mustard seed
1 Tbsp pickling spices
1 Tbsp celery seed
1 Tbsp salt
2 qts vinegar

Add to pickles and let stand overnight. In the morning, heat 35 minutes. Put in pint jars and seal in hot water bath for 15 minutes.

Brown Gravy

2 cups juice from roast or beef broth
3 Tbsp cornstarch with enough water to blend

Add cornstarch mixture to broth. Bring to a boil. Cook until thick. Salt and pepper to taste. (For thicker gravy, add more cornstarch blended with water.)

Pan Gravy

3 Tbsp meat drippings
3 Tbsp flour
2 cups milk or broth

In skillet or roasting pan, add flour to drippings. Blend over low heat until smooth and browned. Add liquid. Cook until mixture boils and thickens, stirring constantly. Salt and pepper to taste. (Use milk as liquid when serving with fried chicken.)

Egg Yolk Noodles

½ cup egg yolks
½ cup evaporated milk
½ tsp salt
2 cups plus 2 Tbsp flour

Beat yolks and add milk. Blend in flour. Knead, roll thin and cut. Dry. Store in freezer.

Photo courtesy of Steve Sell

JOHN DAVID BROWN OF BALDWIN CITY, LEFT, and Kristen Ozbun of Rose Hill, were crowned the homecoming king and queen at McPherson College during half-time ceremonies of the Oct. 3 football game. Brown is a business administration major, with an emphasis in management and finance. He is the son of David and Twilla Brown, Baldwin City. Ozbun is a physical education major. She is the daughter of Brad and Loretta Ozbun, Rose Hill.

Homemade Noodles

2 cups flour
1 tsp salt
½ tsp baking powder
2 eggs
½ tsp butter
5 Tbsp milk

Mix flour, salt and baking powder. Beat eggs, add milk and butter. Combine with flour mixture (will be a stiff dough). Roll out on floured board to very thin. Cut thin strips with a pizza cutter and let dry for 2 or 3 hours. Put in boiling chicken or beef broth. Cook on medium heat 20 to 30 minutes or until done.

Homemade V8 Juice

18 lbs tomatoes
¼ cup onion
1 cup carrots
2 cups celery
⅓ cup sugar
⅛ tsp hot pepper
1 Tbsp celery salt
4 Tbsp salt

Mix together in a large sauce pan. Bring to a boil. Turn
down heat and simmer 40 minutes. Cool. Place in
blender and liquefy.

Punch

(Makes 6 qts)

4 liter bottles of ginger ale, Sprite or 7up
½ gal ice cream sorbet (whatever flavor/color you prefer)

Pour liquid into a punch bowl, then add sorbet.

Kool-Aid Punch

(Makes 3 gallons or 100 cups)

7 pkgs unsweetened Kool-Aid
2 large cans pineapple juice
2 cans frozen lemonade
12 qts water
5 cups sugar

Combine all ingredients. Add 1 large bottle of ginger ale before serving.

MeMe's

FAMILY COOKBOOK

Helen Harrell

Available from Imperium Publishing.

www.imperiumpublishing.com

ISBN 978-1-64318-068-7

IMPERIUM PUBLISHING
CREATE YOUR STORY

Cook Book | U.S. $19.99